M.V.P.
Most Valuable Player

Joe Montana

Bob Italia

Published by Abdo & Daughters, 6535 Cecilia Circle, Edina, Minnesota 55439.

Library bound edition distributed by Rockbottom Books, Pentagon Tower, P.O. Box 36036, Minneapolis, Minnesota 55435.

Printed in the United States.

Cover Photo: Allsport Photography USA, Inc.
Inside Photos: The Bettman Archive: 4, 7, 15, 17, 21, 22, 25, 27, 28, 30.

Edited by Rosemary Wallner

Library of Congress Cataloging-in-Publication Data

Italia, Robert, 1955-
     Joe Montana / written by Bob Italia ; [edited by Rosemary Wallner].
        p. cm. -- (M.V.P. , most valuable player)
Summary: Follows the life of the San Francisco 49ers' quarterback, from his childhood in Pennsylvania through his role in three Super Bowl victories.

ISBN: 1-56239-123-2 (lib. bdg.)

1. Montana, Joe, 1956-   --Juvenile literature. 2. Football players--United States--Biography--Juvenile literature. [1. Montana, Joe, 1956-   --Juvenile literature. 2. Football players.]
I. Wallner, Rosemary, 1964-   . II. Title. III. Series: Italia, Robert, 1955-
M.V.P., most valuable player.
GV939.M59I86   1992
796.332 ' 092--dc20
[B]   92-19753
                                                                        CIP
                                                                        AC

Contents

Joe Montana—The NFL's best quarterback.

The Greatest Quarterback of All Time

There has never been a quarterback like Joe Montana. He has the highest career quarterback rating (94.0). He has the highest career completion percentage (63.9). In four Super Bowl victories, Montana is 83 for 122 with 1,142 passing yards, 11 touchdowns, and *no* interceptions. In those three Super Bowl games, Montana has won the Most Valuable Player award. No one in football has ever won as many.

What's most impressive is his style of play. Montana plays with an intelligence and cool determination that few athletes posses. During his career, Montana has led the San Francisco 49ers to an amazing 23 fourth-quarter comeback NFL victories. No other quarterback in NFL history comes close. It's doubtful anyone will.

Monongahela Joe

Joseph (Joe) Montana, Jr., was born June 11, 1956.
He grew up 30 miles south of Pittsburgh, Pennsylvania,
in a small town called Monongahela (Mo-non-ga-HEE-la).
Monongahela is known for coal mines, steel mills, and
hard-working people. From this tough, competitive,
no-nonsense environment, Montana learned the
values that would one day make him a world-famous
football player.

Montana's mother, Theresa, was a homemaker. His father,
Joseph, Sr., worked at a finance company. Joseph, Sr.,
had a passion for football, and he passed on the love of the
game to his only child.

"I played all sports in the service," Joseph, Sr., recalled.
"But when I was a kid I never had anyone to take me in
the backyard and throw a ball to me. Maybe that's why I
got Joe started in sports. Once he got started, he was
always waiting at the door with a ball when I came home
from work.

"What I really wanted to do was make it fun for him," added
Joe, Sr. "And I wanted to make sure he got the right
fundamentals. I've been accused of pushing him. I don't
think that's right. It's just that he loved it so much, and I
loved watching him. And I wanted to make sure he learned
the right way."

Montana lived in a two-story home in a middle class neighborhood. He was a shy boy and didn't have many friends. When his father worked, Montana practiced throwing a football through a tire hanging from a backyard tree.

When he was only eight years old, Montana played pee-wee football. The age limit was nine. So when his father signed him up, he subtracted a year from Montana's birthday.

Montana receives a kiss from his mother, Theresa,
after winning the MVP award in Super Bowl XVI.

Montana's backyard practicing paid off. His coach, Carl Crawley, noticed Montana's passing talents and started him at quarterback. Montana was an instant success. He played then like he plays now—tough, smart, and determined. Already, he was developing a reputation as a winner.

"We ran a pro offense, with a lot of stuff he's doing now, the underneath stuff," said Crawley. "Joe would roll out. If the cornerback came off, he'd dump it off. If he stayed back, Joe kept going and he'd pick up five or six yards. He was an amazingly accurate passer for a kid.

"Montana had stardom written all over him," Crawley continued. "But nobody ever resented it because it came so naturally. And there was no show-off in him. He wanted to win, and he'd do whatever it took. That's another thing the kids liked about him. With Joe on the field, they knew they were never out of any game."

An All-Around Athlete

Montana did not limit his sports activities to football. He liked playing all sports. "For me, competing in sports was a 365-day-a-year thing," Montana recalled. "I was playing baseball and summer basketball."

Montana played three positions in baseball. In Little League, he pitched three perfect games. But basketball was his favorite sport. He practiced five days a week. His basketball team played in many tournaments around the region.

"Those were the most fun," Montana said. "The trips. We'd go anywhere. One night we played in a tournament in Bethel Park, Pennsylvania, then drove up to Niagara Falls [New York] for another one, then back to Bethel Park for the finals."

Montana played baseball, football, and basketball while at Waverly Elementary School, Finleyville Junior High School, and Ringgold High School. Basketball remained his favorite sport—and he loved to practice. "I could practice basketball all day," he said. Football practice was hard work and not as enjoyable.

At Ringgold High School in 1972, Montana made the varsity team. But he did not start at quarterback. He was 6 feet tall but only weighed 165 pounds. Coach Abramski thought Montana, a sophomore, was too skinny and immature to lead his football team.

Joe vs. Mighty Monessen

In his junior year, Montana took control at mid-season— before the big game at mighty Monessen High School. Monessen was in first place and favored to win the Big Ten league in which Ringgold played.

The big game had all the excitement and pressure of the Super Bowl. Monessen hated Ringgold, and Ringgold hated Monessen. Nobody wanted to lose this game. It would haunt them for the entire year.

"You had to be there," said Keith Bassi, Ringgold's fullback. "I mean Monessen had some players—Bubba Holmes, who went to Minnesota and Tony Benjamin who went to Duke. The rumor was that guys [at Monessen] had been held back a year in nursery school so they'd be more mature when they hit high school.

"We were doing our calisthenics, and there was this big roar," Bassi added. "Here they came—120 of them!—in single file from the top of that concrete stadium, biggest stadium in the [Monongahela] Valley. It was like Custer's Last Stand."

No one gave Ringgold a chance to win. But from the game's beginning, Joe Montana—now taller and bigger— made sure Ringgold wouldn't lose.

Montana displayed the same passing talent he has as a pro. All night long, Montana's passes riddled the Monessen defense. He scrambled left, he scrambled right. Then he set up quickly to toss completions—sometimes through three defenders. He played just like he does today with the San Francisco 49ers. He even celebrated his touchdowns the same way—backpedaling as he threw his hands up.

"They [Monessen] played three-deep, where they give you the short stuff," said Frank Lawrence, Ringgold's offensive line coach. "Joe just killed 'em with timed patterns."

Montana finished the big game with 12 completed passes in 22 attempts for 223 yards. More importantly, he threw four touchdowns. The final score was 34-34. But everyone felt that the underdog Ringgold team had come away with the victory. So had Joe Montana. He would be Ringgold's starting quarterback for the rest of his high school days.

An All-American Quarterback

In his senior year, Montana—now 6 feet 2 inches and 180 pounds—was a star athlete. He could stand flat-footed beneath a hoop, jump, and dunk a basketball with two hands. And he led his basketball team to a championship. As a baseball player, Montana was invited to a major league tryout camp.

Football became Montana's best sport. He quarterbacked his team to an impressive 8-1 regular season. Included in that season was a 44-0 thrashing of Laurel Highlands, and a scrimmage against South Moreland in which Ringgold scored 19 touchdowns! When the football season ended, Montana was named an All-American quarterback.

Montana was a B student in high school. He probably could have done better if he hadn't been so active in sports. He never smoked or drank or even broke curfew.

And he even found time to join the school choir. All his classmates liked him. They chose him class vice president his senior year. Because he was tall and thin with wavy blond hair, Coach Abramski called Montana "Joe Banana."

Colleges everywhere fought to enroll Joe Montana. North Carolina State University offered Montana a basketball scholarship. The University of Notre Dame in South Bend, Indiana, promised he could play basketball *and* football. In all, Montana received a few dozen scholarship offers.

"In his senior year, the [home] games were a happening," said Bob Osleger, Ringgold's golf coach. "There was this flat bit of ground above the stadium, and Joe's father would stand there and watch the game. All these college coaches and scouts would vie for position to stand near him."

Montana visited the University of Georgia, Boston College, the University of Minnesota, Penn State University, the University of Pittsburgh, and Notre Dame. But Montana did it to be polite. He already knew where he wanted to attend college—the University of Notre Dame. His hero, quarterback Terry Hanratty, played for Notre Dame.

"Who's Joe Montana?"

In 1974, eighteen-year-old Joe Montana became engaged to his high school sweetheart, Kim Moses. Then he left Monongahela for South Bend.

Montana quickly discovered that he wasn't Notre Dame's only star athlete. He was rated Notre Dame's eighth-best quarterback and didn't play a single varsity football game. He barely played any of the freshmen games.

Even worse, Montana was homesick. He called his dad four times a week. "The fact is, his father was his best friend," said a former Notre Dame teammate. "The person Joe felt closest to was back in Monongahela."

Montana married Kim Moses during his second semester, then got ready for spring football. Suddenly, the coaches took notice of Montana.

"He had a fine spring practice," said Head Coach Dan Devine, "really outstanding. I came home and told my wife, 'I'm gonna start Joe Montana in the final spring game,' and she said, 'Who's Joe Montana?' I said, 'He's the guy who's going to feed our family for the next few years.' "

The "Comeback Kid"

Despite Devine's prediction, Montana did not start at quarterback his sophomore year. But quarterback Rick Slager was injured in the season's third game against Northwestern University. Montana came in and directed a touchdown drive. Notre Dame won the game 31-7.

Two weeks later, Slager left the North Carolina game with another injury. Notre Dame was losing 14-6 with 5 minutes and 11 seconds left to play. Montana came off the bench and passed for 129 yards in the minute and two seconds on the field—including an 80-yard touchdown that won the game.

The following week, Notre Dame trailed Air Force 30-10 in the fourth quarter. Montana replaced Slager. He led Notre Dame to a 31-30 win. Montana's legend as the "Comeback Kid" was born.

When the 1976 college season began, many people thought twenty-year-old Joe Montana would become Notre Dame's starting quarterback. But Montana separated his shoulder and missed the entire season.

By 1977 Montana, now a junior, was the third-string quarterback. Even worse, Montana's marriage had soured and ended in divorce.

But in the third game of the season against Purdue University, Montana replaced the first two quarterbacks after they could not solve the tough Purdue defense. Purdue led 24-14 with eleven minutes to go. Coach Devine knew what he had to do.

Montana trotted onto the field. The Notre Dame fans cheered wildly. The "Comeback Kid" was at the controls. Purdue didn't stand a chance.

Montana threw for 154 yards and a touchdown. Notre Dame claimed a 31-24 victory. Finally, Montana earned the starting quarterback job. Notre Dame did not lose a game for the rest of the season—and they won a national championship.

Montana performed more comeback magic in 1978. He rallied his team to victory over Pittsburgh and the University of Southern California.

In the 1979 ice-covered Cotton Bowl, Notre Dame trailed the University of Houston 34-12 in the third quarter. Notre Dame won the game with two seconds left as Montana threw an eight-yard touchdown pass. At the time, the victory was called Montana's greatest comeback ever. It was a fitting end to Montana's outstanding college career.

Montana led Notre Dame to a dramatic victory
in the 1979 Cotton Bowl.

Going to California

Despite Montana's legend as the "Comeback Kid," pro scouts did not think he would be a great quarterback. They gave him a 6.5 rating, 9.0 being the best. According to one report: *Montana can thread the needle, but usually goes with his main receiver and forces the ball to him even when he's in a crowd. He's a gutty, gambling, cocky type. Doesn't have great tools but could eventually start.*

Montana graduated from Notre Dame in December. In early 1980, he moved to Manhattan Beach, California, and waited for the National Football League (NFL) draft. Montana wasn't selected until the third round (the eighty-second player overall) by the San Francisco 49ers—one of the NFL's worst teams.

"We were coming off a 2-14 year," said 49er Head Coach Bill Walsh. "We were in dire straits everywhere. I investigated every viable college quarterback. Joe was the last quarterback we looked at. I went down [to the University of California at Los Angeles] to look at him. He worked out with [James] Owens and Theotis Brown, the UCLA fullback who played for Seattle. Joe threw for an hour. The minute I saw him drop back—his quick movement, those quick, nimble, Joe Namath-type feet—I got very serious.

Joe Montana was the 82nd pick in the 1980 NFL draft.

"We looked at films of him in college," Walsh added. "I wanted to see his worst game. At his worst, he played desperate. He'd throw late and beyond the receiver— never early, always late. It's as if he was waiting until the last moment to make something happen.

"At his best," Walsh continued, "he had an instinctive nature rarely equaled by any athlete in any sport. Magic Johnson [former Los Angeles Laker basketball player] has it. But you couldn't lose sight of the fact that he was still a young player. And in game situations, every play is almost crisis-like to a young player."

Montana signed a three-year contract that paid him a base salary of $70,000. When he reported to training camp, his teammates couldn't believe how skinny he was. He only weighed 185 pounds.

Montana started one game his rookie season. Veteran Steve DeBerg was the starting quarterback. Coach Walsh did not want to push Montana too early for fear Montana would lose confidence in himself.

"There were those in our organization who didn't think Joe would be an NFL starter," Walsh said. "That was never even a consideration his first year. I knew the stage he was going through. He was a little in awe of everything, like all first-year quarterbacks. If he hadn't broken out of it, it would have been a different story. But he did break out of it."

In 1980, Montana started seven of the last ten games. He developed a deadly passing attack with tight end Dwight Clark. "We'd stay out after practice and work on our own stuff," Clark said. "I don't know how much it helped him, but it helped me. I didn't have a clue about reading defenses. Joe could. He was good at it."

In a game against New Orleans, Montana rallied the 49ers from a 35-7 deficit to a 38-35 victory. The "Comeback Kid" seemed ready to take on the NFL.

Super Joe

In 1981, Walsh placed the 49ers future on Joe Montana's narrow shoulders. Walsh traded Steve DeBerg and moved Montana into the starting lineup. Walsh, known for his complex offensive strategies, had his system in place. He felt Joe Montana could handle them.

"There was a lot of time spent studying," Montana recalled. " 'Prereads,' we called it—knowing where not to go before the ball was even snapped. You'd learn to work on individuals. Bill's system works only if the guy running the [passing] routes is able to read [defenses].

"Most of our routes have a lot of options built in," he added. "Everyone has to be on the same page. We never want to be at the point where one defense can cover a route completely."

Walsh tailored the 49er offense to Montana's skills. Besides his accurate passing, Montana could throw on the run. Montana used many play action passes—faking a handoff to a running back before rolling out to toss a pass.

Montana ran Walsh's complex offense to near perfection. He led the 49ers to the National Football Conference (NFC) Western Division title. In the NFC championship game against the Dallas Cowboys, the 49ers were down 27-21 with less than five minutes to play.

Montana directed a drive to the Cowboy's six-yard line. There were only fifty-eight seconds remaining, and it was third down. Montana dropped back to pass and spotted Dwight Clark along the back of the end zone. He threw a high soft pass in Clark's direction. Clark leaped high and came down with the ball for a touchdown. The play became known as "The Catch." More importantly, the 49ers had won. They were headed to their first Super Bowl.

"On the touchdown play my concentration level was never so high," Montana said. "I remember pump-faking to get those guys chasing me off the ground, just like when I was playing basketball with my dad. I remember trying to get the ball to Dwight high, so no one else could get it. I never saw the catch. I heard the roar."

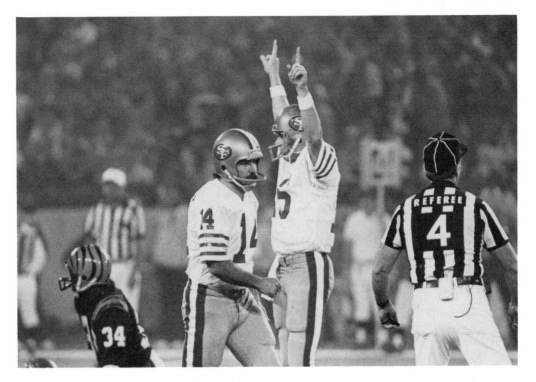

Montana celebrates a score in Super Bowl XVI.

Super Bowl XVI in Pontiac, Michigan, proved to be icing on the cake. Montana guided the 49ers to a 20-0 halftime lead over the Cincinnati Bengals. The 49ers held on for a 26-21 victory. Joe Montana was named the game's Most Valuable Player (MVP).

"Joe Montana will be the great quarterback of the future," Coach Walsh said after the game. "He is one of the coolest competitors of all time, and he has just started."

Montana received a four-year contract worth more than $1.7 million. Endorsement offers came from everywhere.

The next year was an off year for the 49ers. But in 1983, Montana and his team returned to post-season play. They made it all the way to the NFC title game, which they lost 24-21 to the Washington Redskins.

In 1984, the 49ers beat the Chicago Bears in the NFC championship game. Suddenly they found themselves playing the Miami Dolphins and their dazzling quarterback, Dan Marino, in Super Bowl XIX. The game was played at Stanford Stadium in Palo Alto, California. Montana finished the game with 331 passing yards—a Super Bowl record—and three touchdowns as the 49ers won their second Super Bowl, 38-16. Again, Montana received the MVP honor. For being the NFC's top-rated passer, Montana was named to the Pro Bowl team.

Montana is all smiles after receiving
the MVP award in Super Bowl XIX.

"Jen Will You Marry Me?"

Montana had another reason to celebrate in 1984. That year he met Jennifer Wallace. They met while both were filming a Schick razor commercial in New York City. By the summer, Montana was ready to propose marriage. For $600, he hired a plane with a streamer that read: JEN WILL YOU MARRY ME? Then he took Jennifer to her favorite park in San Francisco.

"I looked up, and the streamer was backwards," Montana recalled. "I said, 'Oh, no.' We were on the wrong side of it. I started maneuvering her around. She said, 'Joe, what are you doing?' Finally she saw it. She said, 'Yes,' right away. I was ready for her to say no. Then she said, 'What took you so long?' "

Montana married Wallace in February 1985. They built a home in Redwood City, California. Soon after, their daughter Alexandra was born.

A Pain in the Back

Montana was All-Pro for the 1985 season. But the 49ers lost 17-3 to the New York Giants in the play-offs.

In 1986, Montana had back surgery early in the season. The doctors feared Montana would never play football again.

Montana was determined to return that season. He worked hard to strengthen his back. By November, thirty-year-old Montana was ready for football. In his first game after back surgery, he threw three touchdown passes as the 49ers beat the St. Louis Cardinals 43-17. The 49ers returned to the play-offs, but the New York Giants buried them 49-3.

In 1987, Montana had a career-high 31 touchdown passes. The 49ers finished the regular season with a 13-2 record and were favored to win another Super Bowl. But the Minnesota Vikings shocked the 49ers in San Francisco, 36-24. During the game, Montana had been benched. Because of his back problems, people wondered if Montana was on the decline.

The Best Ever?

In 1988, Montana shared the quarterback job with Steve Young. Coach Walsh labeled Young as the 49ers future starting quarterback. When the team reached the play-offs, Walsh started Montana because of his experience.

It was a wise decision. Montana led his team to Super Bowl XXIII in Miami, Florida. In the game, Montana rallied the 49ers over the Cincinnati Bengals 20-16. With only 34 seconds left, Montana completed eight of nine passes during a 90-yard touchdown drive. The 49ers had won their third Super Bowl in as many appearances.

Montana strikes a famous pose in Super Bowl XXIII.

It was the 19th time as a professional football player that Joe Montana had brought his team from behind and led it to victory in the fourth quarter. Instead of criticizing Montana, sportswriters everywhere said he was one of the best quarterbacks ever.

"Joe Montana is not human," Cincinnati wide receiver Cris Collingsworth said after the game. "I don't want to call him a god...he's somewhere in between."

How does he do it? How does Joe Montana continually rally his team to victory?

"Maybe it's because ever since I was little I was involved in pressure situations, plus winning traditions," Montana said, referring to his youthful athletic days in Monongahela. "You knew you had to win. Those basketball tournaments we played in—Niagara Falls one night, Bethel Park the next night—you learned to deal with it.

"What I want is the chance to play, to compete," he added. "When a coach would sit you down, when you knew you'd get yanked if you didn't do well, that was real pressure. Once you know you can play no matter what, then the pressure is only what you create for yourself."

In 1989, Coach Walsh quit as 49er Head Coach. Many thought the new coach, George Siefert, could not bring the 49ers back to the Super Bowl. But Montana had the best year ever for a quarterback as he completed more than 70 percent of his passes with 26 touchdowns.

The 14-2 49ers found themselves in Super Bowl XXIV at the Superdome in New Orleans, Louisiana. Montana threw five touchdown passes—a Super Bowl record—as the 49ers won 55-10 over the Denver Broncos. It was the biggest rout in Super Bowl history. And the 49ers became the first team since the Pittsburgh Steelers (1979 and 1980) to win back-to-back Super Bowls.

Montana scrambles to another victory in Super Bowl XXIV.

Montana receives The Sporting News
1989 Man of the Year *award with his wife, Jennifer.*

Montana became the first three-time MVP award winner. Now there was no doubt that Joe Montana was the best quarterback ever.

In the 1990 season, 34-year-old Joe Montana finished with the third-highest rating for a quarterback in the NFC. He wanted to win a third-consecutive Super Bowl—something no team has ever done.

Montana led the 49ers to the NFC Championship game against the New York Giants. Montana hurt his thumb during the game and Steve Young replaced him. The 49ers were not the same. Though the 49ers led 14-13 in the fourth quarter, the Giants won 16-14 on a last-minute field goal. Had Montana played the entire game, it may have ended differently.

One More Comeback?

In August 1991, Montana injured his elbow while throwing a pass. The 49ers had to start the football season without him. Montana hoped to be back before the season ended. But then he decided to have elbow surgery. With quarterback Steve Young, the 49ers didn't make the play-offs. In San Francisco, people wondered if the "Comeback Kid" could make one more comeback.

*Despite his injuries, Montana isn't ready
to say goodbye to the game he loves.*

"I'll be the one to know when I shouldn't play anymore," Montana said. "People always want to retire athletes before their time, but that's not going to happen to me. Nobody's going to get me to go sooner than I want to. As long as I love doing the job, feel like I can do the job, I'm *going* to do the job."

No one should be surprised by Montana's determined attitude. Comebacks are this fiery competitor's specialty. Sore elbow and all, Joe Montana will be back with the San Francisco 49ers.

The Private Side of Joe Montana

When not on the football field, Joe Montana likes to spend time with his family. Besides daughter Alexandra, Joe and Jennifer have daughter Elizabeth and son Nathaniel to care for.

"There are two sides to Joe," said Jennifer, "the one people see on the field and the one we see at home. What makes him comfortable is his home and his kids and everyday life, not being put on a pedestal, not being called a hero every five minutes."

Now that he has a four-year, $13 million contract, Montana has limited his endorsements and speaking engagements. But he still finds time to do community service and charity work.

As for life after football, Montana already has plans. "I'd like to go up to the northern California wine country and settle down," he said. "Open a little Italian restaurant with seven or eight or ten tables and a big wine list. I'd like to own some vineyard land, grow my own grapes, make wine. I'd also like to work with kids, like my dad did."

Whatever he decides to do, Joe Montana will be a great success. It's all he's ever known.

Joe Montana's Address

You can write to Joe Montana at the following address:

Joe Montana
c/o The San Francisco 49ers
711 Nevada St.
Redwood City, CA 94061